DESIGNED FOR FLIGHT

Also by Gregory Fraser

DESIGNED FOR FLIGHT

Poems

GREGORY FRASER

TRIQUARTERLY BOOKS/NORTHWESTERN UNIVERSITY PRESS
EVANSTON, ILLINOIS

TriQuarterly Books
Northwestern University Press
www.nupress.northwestern.edu

Printed in the United States of America

10 9 8 7 6 5 4 3 2 1

Library of Congress Cataloging-in-Publication Data
Fraser, Gregory, author.
    [Poems. Selections]
    Designed for flight : poems / Gregory Fraser.
        pages cm.
    ISBN 978-0-8101-5243-4 (pbk. : alk. paper)
    I. Title.
PS3606.R423A6 2014
813.6—dc23

                                                                2013039096

∞ The paper used in this publication meets the minimum requirements of the American National Standard for Information Sciences—Permanence of Paper for Printed Library Materials, ANSI Z39.48-1992.

for Milada, David, and Sasha

CONTENTS

III

IV

ACKNOWLEDGMENTS

My gratitude to the editors of the following journals:

American Literary Review: "The Good Life," "Not a Word"

Birmingham Poetry Review: "Ficus," "If Only," "Spitting Image"

Five Points: "At the Degas Exhibit," "First Mortgage"

The Gettysburg Review: "The End," "Rainbow, Rainbow, Rainbow," "Splotches"

Hotel Amerika: "Correspondent"

Iron Horse Literary Review: "Alternative Contours of Space and Time," "First Night Alone with Twins," "Lingo," "The Theft"

The Missouri Review (online): "The Great Northeast"

New South: "Love to Death," "Marriage"

North American Review: "Judeophilia"

Poetry East: "Menelaus"

Scythe: "Bread," "Instructions for Assembling a Nation," "Prodigal Son"

Southern Indiana Review: "Ending with a Line from a Travel Guide," "Ohio in Late Summer," "Springfield"

Southern Poetry Review: "Her Mistake"

Sou'wester: "Orpheus & Co.," "The Stuff"

Tampa Review: "Man of Feeling"

The Texas Review: "White Night on the Neva"

32 Poems Magazine: "The Lord's Prayer"

Waccamaw: "After the Miscarriage," "To a Fool"

"Ficus" and "Love to Death" were republished on *Verse Daily.* "The Lord's Prayer" appears in *Old Flame: From the First 10 Years of 32 Poems Magazine* (Seattle: WordFarm, 2013). "The Stuff" was reprinted in *The Southern Poetry Anthology,* vol. 5, Georgia (Huntsville: Texas Review Press, 2013).

Thanks to David Bottoms, Eric Elshtain, David and Barbara Fraser, Michael Griffith, David Hartley, Jane and Robert Hill, Edward Hirsch, Tamara Marenkova, Corey Marks, Susannah Mintz, David Newton, Lisa Propst, Megan Sexton, Dave Smith, Adam Vines, Laurie Watel, Eleanor Wilner, and Amanda Yskamp. Special gratitude to my editor, Mike Levine, and the staff at Northwestern University Press, as well as to Chad Davidson and Christine Sneed for their invaluable help with this book.

DESIGNED FOR FLIGHT

I

The Great Northeast

If they still botch grammar in Northeast Philly,
      Lord, let's leave it that way, at least on the corner
            where Givens Market sat on its thumb.

The door sign lacked possessive punctuation,
      belying the trove inside: musks of garlic and armpits,
            towers of powdered milk, deviled ham.

Eight to eight, the storefront gaped from thick
      glass blocks—6 x 6 inch cubes frozen by fire—
            at the joust of Howard and West Courtland,

jostle of white kids and black, almost guiltless
      indigents and Rizzo's thugs. Pimpled, scrawny,
            greasy-haired, I would palm a Red Delicious

then scurry home to sprawl in my parents' bed
      and marvel as the Broad Street Bullies bloodied ice
            on a black-and-white no larger than lunch—

just as I had opened for the fuzzy tube
      to feed me Vietnam, toy-sized soldiers
            scudding brush. Mrs. Given lisped,

her husband hauled on his back
      a lump absurd as the acorn squash
            that never sold, and I—surrogate boy,

sweet un-son, given to unctuousness
      and theft—bagged and shelved
            to the FM spilling *Baby, how long*

will you keep me in the penalty box?
    The Cup that year stayed home, so number 8
        kept crooning. It strikes me now my father,

whose take-home every month went straight
    to banks, might have trilled the same refrain,
        only *Baby* would call up men in worsted suits—

as in, *Yeah, Baby, like that, do me like that.*
    This, understand, well before I scanned
        anything but "The Raven" and "The Road

Not Taken," flubbed by nuns, but sweet Son
    of Man, I see today: if a hockey enforcer
        like Dave "The Hammer" Schultz could belt

out public song, why couldn't I—if only
    from the smooth white rink of a page?
        And if the evening star were a tooth

punched clean from the mouth of Billy Penn
    poised atop City Hall, if my soft employers
        survived the Hat Trick Reich, were given

a second chance to sniff cantaloupes for ripeness,
    what could it matter to skip an apostrophe
        that lisps *I own this, this is mine*? Better to go

on dredging years in flour, serve up
    something in truth and barely claim it.
        Even if it's a fist to the lip of Denis Potvin

or a store's hand-lettered sign. Why else
    did the glaciers open envelopes of stone?
        So we could read time's invitation

and answer with an ardent *Yes, I shall attend.*
        Why else would Mrs. Given press a twenty
                in my palm at Christmas, a holy day for which

she could not bend? No wonder they call it
        The Great Northeast. No wonder at all.
                Old neighborhood, I spit this on the ice for you.

First Mortgage

I still catch the spindles of the kitchen chairs,
family spaniel begging scraps. In the window
dusk slowly hoists its scrim on pulleys.

I am eight, past Communion, as my father
slits the mail, stacks bills, then bangs his gavel
of a fist against his brow, trying to restore

some form of order. The cheap Sylvania
mumbles in the corner—something *jungle,*
something *Rouge.* Checkered porch light

through the lattice. And now my mother
reaches past me, through me, I am
transparent, rests her hand on top of his.

Not for a moment do I think to place my own
on hers, and add what solace I might
against their far campaigns. That evening I can only

drop my chin (shuffle of foot soles, whimper
from the favorless dog) and spot the napkin
on my lap: starched, ironed, inconceivably blank.

At the Degas Exhibit

The docent wends us to *The Dance Class*
and it all flits back: the studio downtown,
few bucks an hour, ragging off the finger

grease of toe-shoed cygnets, tutu-ed swans,
who glided hardwood blind to both
of me—spray of acne, high-top Keds.

I would clatter on the local after school
(weekends once the Christmas pageant neared),
my face, at every stop, floating outside

the window by my seat—a mask
tried on by stars in movie ads, commuters
cooling heels for later cars. Then Windex,

buff, till six, waving *hello, farewell,*
from glass to glass, plié to pointe—my hand
emitting squeaks, eliding dainty prints and streaks.

In my knapsack: comics, *Catcher,* lunch
untouched. And never once did I happen on
the courage even to speak to one of those

sugarplums of Rittenhouse, Society Hill.
Degas's girls, our guide informs, practice
attitudes, inspected by their master

(one Jules Perrot) propped on his staff.
Note the Parisian mothers dabbed
on the wall in back. Yet I see only tights

that bear the stamp *Massey Dance,* hear
gripes about third position, giddy talk
of boys, and search the sides and corners

for my Old World counterpart—some
sponge-and-bucket kid from a ragged edge—
undersized, nearsighted, invisible to art.

Lingo

In the scratch and shuffle of the fifteenth year,
black at the nail, unsung, you and your closest friend
shuck corn for Sunday supper on his nana's porch.
The shy one, you, shoos flies and mothers a zit,

while Danny dreams out loud—tearing open ears,
chucking husks in a produce crate—of peeling off
the jeans and daisied undies of Joanne Walker
to tickle her blond silk and hear her moan.

He bandies slang like *snatch, poonany, gooch*—
which sound more to you like the penny-ante games,
full of wild cards and kooky rules, your father dealt
whenever mother stranded him with kids—

and speaks of working his finger like a feather,
slowly, gently at first, then jackhammer quick,
until she begs him never to quit. Through an open
window the soon-to-be commander in chief

of the great U.S. of A. greatly communicates
from his gilded stump, as Danny Gallagher ponders
(having lately raided his granddad's stash of smut)
the wonders of Joanne's *beaver, cha-cha, muff.*

You nod and flash approving grins, but only
to keep him talking while you think of her and you
the afternoon before, meeting in woods behind
her house, to impress a mattress of moldered leaves,

lock lips, practice French, and run from
first to second base and back, time after time.
Willows pouted at the pond line, a catbird
harassed a squirrel, and Joanne said nothing

of him, her official steady. You were strangers
glued by her fear of getting *knocked up,*
preggers, yours of being marked a *fag,*
the prospect more unnerving since the initials

of your name (Gregory Allen Fraser, say)
spelled terror in reverse. Traitor and tramp, seraph
and hostess of heaven, swapping spit and awkward
silence, you kept hands above the beltline,

which was all you needed just then. Meanwhile,
Danny planned ahead, mastering the mix of raunchy lingo
and straight-toothed American brio bound to impress
the guys already smoking dope and peeling out

in tricked-out cars, and win Joanne for good.
But that would have to wait till autumn, when school
resumed its candied falsehoods. For now, as the porch swing
squeaks in the breeze, Danny murmurs in the backdrop—

hoo ha, nana, biscuit—and no grandmother chirps
anyone in to eat, you savor the moment behind the moment,
as Joanne tears away her mouth to brand your neck
with a small red circle (very small)—a mark that makes you

both forget, for a gnat-bitten instant, you are growing up
in a town with one high school, one hospital, and one moon,
spinning and rattling off each summer month, like a hubcap
lost on a bend of night—a town only one of you escapes.

Ice

We drove out under starlight,
a hearse of circus clowns,
passed a fifth, spat at the sky.
And groaned about the bloodless
proofs of math, a father's strop,
the prim napkins some sister
folded cleverly to stand
erect. The moon beat its face
against the water tower, phone
wires stretched east and west
like frozen nerves. Later,
bored and loaded, we pulled
on skates and slapped a puck
till we doubled over, gasping.
Then one guy flipped
around his stick, took aim,
and opened fire. We blasted
until every man lay cold.

Memory

His name, Andrew, his recall, total, we dragged him everyplace.
At Wilson's Pond, we aimed him at turtles humping, a hawk
undressing a vole. You could almost hear a shutter snap.
One Saturday: all of us down cellar, melting army men
on cold cement—two floors from dad and mom doing, you know,
the horizontal cha-cha. With soldiers from both sides fused
in a blue-green blob (the stench worse than singed arm hair),
we called for Andrew to document, but he was nowhere in sight.
In the kitchen stood mom and dad, sheepish and peeved,
tightening their robes. *Where's Andrew?* we wondered. *Home.*

Were I to dial Andrew up today, I could hear my bowling scores,
frame by frame, from the summer of '74. Pinball tallies, batting
and earned-run averages. I used to wish for his photographic
memory, but what I really wanted was a photogenic one.
I remember my screwups best, in vivid, wrenching detail—
like the time I called a neighbor *dirty pinko* to her face
(turns out she was Jewish and barely escaped). Why shouldn't
my sins, if set to haunt me, at least flaunt rakish good looks?

Last I heard, Andrew dumped accounting to track down peace
in Oregon or Washington State. Someone said he flew out West
on business, fell for rugged seascapes. Others claim the visions
of Ansel Adams—peopleless, severe—made him drive to Yosemite
and ditch his car. Truth is, he could be anywhere, anyone—
an operative for the CIA, or hot-dog vendor on Seventh Ave.,
a preschool teacher or jewel thief entranced by his hoard.
I lean toward the latter, because every so often at a family picnic

or holiday meal, my father glances at mom and wonders out loud
to the group, *Whatever happened to Andrew?* From the look
on my parents' faces, it is clear my friend walked off
with something of theirs, something priceless they still want back.

The Theft

A few weeks into first semester
at the central Pennsylvania college
I partied myself out of
in less than a year, I stole
my roommate's girlfriend with a kiss
one starless night outside our dorm—
or put more truly, she threw a leg across
and borrowed me, like an unchained
bike, to ride away from him.
Even though she dropped me, too,
not long after—or let's say
she leaned me gently against
a tree—it nags me to this day
that he packed for the family farm,
never returned. Thirty years and still
I picture him behind the wheel
(sky the color of denim, horses
in the distance, grazing on the distance),
cursing me every mile from school
to home. Her name was Judy, his, Eric,
I can't remember mine. I can call up
little more than ramen soups, stacked
higher than books on our shelves, the guitar
I picked at all the time, a musical scab,
and his scuffed-up golf clubs in the corner
(he'd made the team with ease).
He scrawled ASSHOLE in Magic Marker
on my book bag before he left,
and of course I couldn't blame him
but blamed him all the same,

telling the guys on the floor
what a rube he was, a yokel,
until he entered our collective memory,
then our communal forgetting. Judy,
I have no doubt, runs a law firm now,
her dark eyes trained on justice,
and some nights, awake in bed,
I think of Eric as a tall, thick-wristed kid
just out of high school, who could drive
a tractor, track a deer, and knock
a golf ball farther than any man
for a hundred miles. In my dream for him,
he keeps his feelings locked inside
a cabin in the woods, but lets them out
at last—stunned and blinking—
when he meets the perfect woman
(what would you say?) working
the ticket booth at a summer fair.
But other times, when dreams won't do,
I fear he married the girl he took
to prom. They get on fine, steadily
if blandly, raise some kids, until the day
the vision returns, and Eric sees himself
at the second-story window, peering
down at Judy and me, leaning close.
That's when, in disgust, he grits
his teeth and throws a hand
in the air, dismissing the life he chose
with the gesture of a golfer
tossing up a pinch of grass
to test the inclination of the wind.

Judeophilia

You trace it to Jaime Slotsky of the auburn hair,
        her voice half helium, half phlegm, nose and forearms
                constellated with fizzled suns. She the first to dare

a goy to supper of boiled beef, potatoes pummeled
        flat and fried, beets that tinted your piss to rose water,
                diluted blood. Clouds of flour, Welch's and wine,

Chagall's *I and the Village* above, Promised Land candles on
        the mantel, and you kept silence like a vigil—
                you curio, you spy—sopping up the thin brown juice

and mash of Yiddish, Russian, broken English,
        unable to conjure Babel, or any tri-tongued hound
                underground, for Classics waited grades ahead.

And when the Slotskys spread instead
        of tucked their napkins, called each other
                many names, yukked and poked at sides, and spoke

without reserve of Him—His fickleness, His absence,
        His grief—each speech pregnant with others, you knew
                yourself one of them already and never one, a wanderer

among the wayward, equally designed for flight,
        as stubby fingers stabbed at air, or wagged in refutation,
                nein, nyet, no. What to do but side with Jaime's cousin,

on scholarship at Penn, claiming human spirits
        the same as stars, fragments of the first great light;
                with her uncle Sol, as well—*Pass the pickles, salt,*

the bread—quoting Moshe and Buber (local plumbers,
  for all you knew); with Jaime's mother, too, who chimed
    above the jabber, "Dessert, everyone, dessert."

And how to keep from staring at, or turning from,
  the one they all called *Bube*, seated to your right:
    balding, hunched, in a quiet wholly different

from your own? You showed then
  at the door each afternoon—anomalous,
    malodorous, refugee from the bookless,

pest or pet, no one bothered to decide—to nibble Chex
  from the bag, Kedem biscuits and Tam Tam crackers,
    snuggle next to Jaime and watch the *Match Game*

and *Tattletales* on a couch cocooned in plastic
  you nearly slid off, time and again, into what?
    Nothing your own neighborhood could fathom,

with its buckled asphalt, stillborn winds,
  its taproom chapel and stifled lexicon of *hymie,*
    hebe. Or everything, perhaps, that poor Catholic block

understood, after older sons and brothers, raised
  in the crosshairs of Oakford Road and Aubrey Ave.,
    were blasted to Vietnam to swallow beans and dicks

and scamper boonies, praying never
  to snuggle in body bags. Thereafter, too,
    you spent weekends in your room (Clearasil

on the bed stand, confirmation pin; Bobby Clarke
  and Farrah Fawcett facing off from opposing walls;
    lava lamp in sanguinary dream) using pliers to twist

the nub of the TV knob from network
        to PBS, gnawing commas of dead skin off
                your fingers' ends. There were heaps of bones

you took at first for shoes; gloves and boots
        polished to a glare that weirdly thrilled. In wonder,
                shock, pajamas or T-shirt and jeans, you studied

the drilled, uniform steps at rallies, who had witnessed
        only Mummers on parade—kooky peacocks strumming
                banjos, swigging Schlitz, a harmless ruckus down Broad

each New Year's Day. And before you knew—
        revenant zipped in costume skin—you had risen
                from arson at the Reichstag and Commies rounded up

to der Führer's eye shift and stare, His trousers
        puffed, to march with no goofy kazoo across
                your own deep sleep—an arm thrust at the angle

of evil, then stretched with palm upturned,
        feeding Chex to a painted goat. And so you were,
                and were not, one of them, as well. Now

crooked cross, now six-tipped star, one
        strapped to your left, the other to your right
                upper arm, and you unsure how the same amount

of stitching sorted the defiled and pure.
        Who in the world to ask? Not Jaime who wanted
                to play Rod Stewart, over and over, in her room,

or sneak to voiceless woods, half undress
        and grope (you should never have forsaken
                the three nests she built for you, under her arms

and between her thighs; never would you flap,
a mad bird, among them). Not her father, or yours,
whose lessons always ran: *When your one death*

staggers out of hills, roams in search of you,
rubbing its clear gray eyes, know which streets
double back and assume false names. No—

your only source was *Bube,* with alleys
of Odessa in her heels, horrid calculus
up one sleeve. Yet how to approach, address?

What could you even tally of her? That she rarely
spoke, and always in a tongue that boxed your ears?
That she hummed whenever she mopped or swept,

and clearly adored Chagall—flash of spring,
a childscape, damp little births in hovels, cows
here steady, there dazed. Was she even human? Or,

from the first, one of those unsuspecting angels
stripped naked by a raving god and raped back
into flesh? *Nein.* That her head was as gray

as the end of winter, making her the death
of death, which is new life? *Nyet.* That she dreamed
each wound could heal like water, without a scar,

and wished the flags of nations only red
and black, yellow and brown—the color of hair? *No.*
What did it even matter, to you who looked away,

sensing she watched and somehow knew
what you wondered and wished to ask,
until she stood one day to face you—

her far eyes to your four, your scrawny
          forearm to her inked—and invite you over
                    for seder. *Run home,* she said in English

shockingly clear, *and come tomorrow*
          before the sun has set. She had already
                    read your mind, shut its thin, untitled volume,

shelved it for later use, and suspected
          what you'd spit, stupidly at table: *goddamned*
                    Nazis, or some such truck. If you came at all.

Outside, a dusk-gray moth caromed off
          the porch lamp, prompting you to fly, and you
                    washed down walks like ash, castaway thoughts

of fire, jubilant and scared, holding in
          your head her invitation to a rite never
                    chalked on the board at school. You didn't show.

Who knows what you did instead. Tuned in
          to *Sanford and Son? Chico and the Man?*
                    Or simply slipped into the coma of flipping

through *TV Guide?* And then it was summer
          and Jaime's *Bube* was dying. Then she was
                    lately dead—so you heard, though not

from the henna girl. (That her heart was the size
          and darkness of a nail hole, where a sun-blanched
                    photo of import used to hang; or a knot

in a pinewood plank, spot from which a living
          branch once reached? That she could not weep
                    openly after the purge, but lamented still—

invisibly, impossibly slowly—like leaded glass?)
        What sham hypotheses you hatched. What
                regrets, for years, treaded sleep. You should never

have let the grass redden in their yard
        without you, should have snapped the thread
                that blinds the needle. And what a tiny branding

you feared: *Jew lover, kike kisser.*
        You kiss on the cheek, you halo, noose—dumb
                Catholic kid, with so much history on his side.

II

Rainbow, Rainbow, Rainbow

While you listed out my faults, I
listened in such complete
agreement my mind felt free
to roam—first to the mirror's unbroken
tablet, then out the window to houses
on our block, their roofs like books
splayed open, facedown, half read.

Your reasons for suggesting we
quit, every one compelling, gently
explained, inspired me to peer
through the portal of night
at the pale blue stone on which you
arced overhead like a rainbow.
Everyone likes a rainbow, and surely

I liked you. Perhaps your name was
Rainbow. Your comments might
have oppressed me, like a low ceiling
or yard spread with feces of geese,
but you let me down easy, with lots
of padding, as professional movers will
an antique chest. This made me

less inclined to fashion
a second record of my flaws,
or brood on further misfortunes.
It never occurred to me, for instance,
to worry that I'd stopped reading
living poets, and lost the bulk
of my friends, or that another man

was leasing the inside of my head,
with its glorious acoustics,
to practice tortured arias.
I have been meaning to thank you
for a while, and mail off
an equally tender and perceptive
ledger of your unique shortcomings,

but you know how time flies in
circles, Rainbow, riding thermals
then swooping for a kill, and how
sluggishly it lifts off after feeding,
wings as heavy and awkward as
some makeshift design by Daedalus
in his rush to master flight.

Orpheus & Co.

He staggered all night through the streets alone,
ending up on an esplanade at dawn, where he watched
the night respire, fogging the river's glass. Once,

during introductions on New Year's Eve, you paused
too long before my name, and I understood,
in an instant, your restlessness for a separate life.

He thought about Eurydice's hand extended,
inches from his grasp, and the vision, like a riptide,
pulled him deeper into their past. After, we found

our windshield glazed with frozen rain. I fired
the motor, got down to work with the scraper,
then pressed a gloved palm to the windshield

when the view came clear. He could see himself
and her, hidden in grass, tilting back their heads
to taste the rain, then dropping to sleep by the cadence

of each other's breaths. Instead of holding up
your hand to mine, you frantically waved me inside
the car, shouting, *Hurry, goddammit, it's freezing.*

They say he could charm the beasts and fish,
coax rocks to dance, divert a river's course, bend
the will of gods. Yet anxiously he turned and down

she slid. And when the two of us split at last,
chasing clouds across the plains, I also mourned.
But that was years ago, and far from the rapid Hebrus.

The Good Life

It called to us in the raspy notes of jays,
melodies of warblers and wrens, but we idled

side by side at trolley stops, noses wedged
in earnest books, or earphones tuned

to broadcasts mainly grim. It mailed out
invitations from the stationery stores

of wasps, which peddle the finest papers,
but we were in the midst of moving, and left

no future address. We griped that all the carnivals
had folded, the gray canvas tents of skies

slackening on lawns, while the good life
set off flares—the crack of a bat and deep fly ball

streaking over the fences, sprinklers ignited
at dawn. It welcomed with outstretched arms,

big eyes pooled with light, but we were always
gazing elsewhere, studying the hills gone mad

on bed rest, the willow with its lovely tresses,
awful stoop. And when we finally turned

to face it, the good life had given up
on us (understandably by then, old love)

and settled for another couple—more open
to its windows, less wary of the glass.

Ending with a Line from a Travel Guide

Some nights before I drop to sleep
I summon up your hair, snapping
with wind on top of Arthur's Seat,
stuffed beneath a Yankees cap,
or clumped inside the drain—me
on the tile with a monkey wrench,
straining to loosen the nut, unclog
the trap. I remember hours cupped
in hands entwined across the table,
a yellow raincoat cheering the foyer.
But then recall how hard we searched
to find, let alone share, a middle ground,
how the two of us wrapped ourselves
in woolen sweaters of routine.
I prefer to watch us scale the bluffs
overlooking Dunsapie Loch, or shriek
for Mattingly to smack one out
of the park, but the late hour shadows
the view. I see us again, in love
but drifting, afraid if we speak
our tongues will turn to scalpels,
words to incisions impossible to stitch.
I am not sure how we stayed attentive,
so present to each other, really,
given all our errors and omissions.
Yet tonight, as the moon canoes across
my window, I do not want an answer.
I want to shut my eyes and let us
paddle the Water of Leith, your hair
unruly, my nerves in check, the river
like a silver thread in a ribbon of green.

Ohio in Late Summer

We loathed the state with silent passion,
even if we longed, years later, to return,
as some revisit sites of wreckage
for the wide-aired, eerie calm.

Afternoons we sat engrossed
by the chipmunks' lessons
in burial; when dusk drove light
from the lawn, we rode to fields

of corroded steel; and one time,
you must recall, wound arm in arm
to the quarry, as bats took jagged
flight, and the gash of sunset healed.

I eulogized our metropolis of art,
you lamented lost fashion and food,
and we said out loud—the first time
it seemed—how trapped we felt

in open space. Then, though not our style,
we stripped and lowered into the lake.
Summer still held on, but the water chilled.
We treaded and shivered—heads like tops

of icebergs above the surface—and went
on and on about the need for escape,
as if complaint could somehow warm us,
as if our talk were even of the place.

Springfield

The faucet in the kitchen mocked us,
its steady pulse a gibe at our erratic rhythms,
and in the distance, farmland stretched
like corduroy—furrowed, dry.
Somehow though we managed three
winters' glassy cracklings, the two-way
county roads with dotted lines
like coupons unredeemed.
You recollect, I'm sure, the sound
that morning I turned the ignition
after the starter froze. Time did anything
but pass with that same flurry of clicks.
Evenings the wind curled up in trees,
turning only once or twice in sleep.
You'd think it might be easy, surrounded
by so little motion, to light a match.
Yet our bodies, no matter how we tried,
joined like pieces from different puzzles—
awkwardly, with small, unsightly gaps.
One day your hair cascading,
the next dammed up in a bun.
Wines of black currant infused with peat.
And then they began to stack—
the doubts, regrets—like cordwood.
If only we could have stoked an ember
beneath the surface ash. We might
have torched the entire stock.

Spitting Image

Your perfect likeness sat across from me today,
crossing town on the express, and all at once
I was yours again, you mine. The woman—
middle forties, temples daubed with ash—
spread the city on her lap, and we
were trading dreams and miseries again
on a street in Queens—the sky crosshatched
with vapors, ubiquitous jets. Her finger
drifting north to Morningside Heights
brought back the soot, incessant on sills,
and jack-o'-lantern smiles of electric storms
we waved away but feared. For an instant
the train lights blinked, an instant later
our glances caught, and because this is not
mathematics, not Bridge or bridge construction,
I rose and took the seat beside her, apologized
for my ruses and pranks. I told her
I still think about the two of us back then,
nimbly climbing latticed expectations,
recalled the time we rode the rail
to Montauk, stood in surf and parsed
the zodiac's white lies. Was that the night
I began to sort you, deciding which parts
to keep, which to feed to fat-mouthed stars?
Had you made up your mind to suggest
I shove off? Soon, this spitting image of you
reached her stop, slipped out into the throng.
I could have followed her onto the platform,
up the steps to blinding midday, could have
tapped an elbow and proposed we grab a bite.
But with all the restaurants in town, it always
took forever (you remember) to agree on one.

Her Mistake

When cinders showed up in her blouses,
cacti in her platelets, siroccos inside
her compact mirror, when she started to read
with the little white eyes of old potatoes,
and speak in basso profundo—distant
and godlike—as if through a sewage pipe,
she knew the time had come.
Like the finch, she did her knitting in
corners, like the squirrel got very drunk
on hoarding for bleaker seasons.
She fangled a cap of colored wools
to ward off snowy absence, and buried,
with paws bark-sharpened, cherished gauds—
by the sweet-gum tree his laugh, nose
by the climbing rose. When she found
on her fork a clump of dirt and nearly
gulped it, when a reconditioned mattress
and box spring floated in a casket
down a river of dream, she was certain
they'd dissolve by September's end.
Her mistake. They stuck it out
an extra month, then she helped him
pack, load up boxes, and they watched
the diggers in gray, one last time
out the kitchen window, stock up for a winter
predicted to freeze the blood.

Ficus

The morning he drove off, she pretended
not to notice, not to feel like a dope
shoving food in her mouth, half chewing
on her hands. At the pantry window
she listened to the grackle's transformational
grammar, the sapsucker's Morse code,
believing their messages unchanged.
She studied the unmown lawn, imagined
grass first nibbled in Eden, then pondered
death, napping in the cramped quarters
of jackknives and bullet chambers,
or snoring in an unforeseen pandemic.
These distractions, for a time, worked
wonders. But then she recalled the way
he talked about the bleached period
of the moon, running around in search
of a sentence to end. Perhaps she should
never have insisted it was wrong
to keep butterflies and angels out of poems.
Can you blame them now, she'd asked,
for refusing invitations? That morning
as he pulled away, she convinced herself
he was headed out on errands, despite
the crates of clothes and books crammed
in the trunk, the potted ficus in the back.
Then, late afternoon, it struck her—the lushness
of the plant, blocking his rearview mirror.

The Squall

Driving from the house and life they built,
after holding her an hour, bidding a proper
good-bye, was the hardest thing he never did.
The turnpike south to Albany was vacant,
he was an antihero in search of plot,
and right at the border of Pennsylvania,
snow began its edits and elisions—
so dense he had to exit, find a motel.
The curtains in the room were ghastly
(she would have glared at them in shock),
and when he pulled the cord, they opened
on the portrait of their future apart. Of course,
he loved her still, enough to close the script
of their tender charade. He would never
excuse himself for setting out after
too few words, just as he would never
forget the squad of boys, spotted through
the squall that day, chasing a puck
down the Delaware, which earlier he
had crossed to the banks of another life.

Alternative Contours of Space and Time

The day I shambled into manhood, neon
at the local pub flashed SULL VAN'S, the dead
"I" like a tooth knocked out in a brawl
dives like that were famous for,
though this one wasn't. Dusk slid down
the window in front, and I still see a carpenter,
claw hammer snug in its holster,
a postman at the end of the bar, working
the crossword. Had Brueghel painted the scene,
he would have placed an idiot boy at a sink
in back, washing mugs with a ratty brush.
How often, in our dozen years, three states,
did I fashion myself into that hidden kid,
missing letter in the taproom sign, or any
of the unmarked squares in the mailman's puzzle?
No surprise we never quite aligned: you decapitating
carrots in the kitchen, or lifting from a vase
daisies tinged with rust, while I boarded a bus
then pulled the chain for my stop—a nexus
for which no crossroads exist. The world
of feeling may be ruled by different physics,
alternative contours of space and time,
but finally our grievances and joys obeyed
the standard laws—shrinking with greater distance
and reacting to the speeds and paths
of outside forces (your imperative yoga
class, my hours lost to drink) in ways both
opposite and equal. I can only thank the stars
I had the sense to leave—or did you force me
to throw myself out? No matter. The first months
were sleepless, dull, eyeholes drilling the dark.

But somehow I found passage out, and though
I did come close, avoided ending up alone
and unself-conscious, pathetically so, like that still
unmarried philosophy prof at every school
that gave us jobs—the one who throws a party
to close each year, and like centuries of weather
over limestone, wears down all his guests
with proofs against or for a realm beyond the skies,
until he winds up in his den, well before
midnight, with half-empty plates of snacks,
a plaster bust of Augustine or Nietzsche,
and the muffled groans in the background
of one lingering undergrad, too wasted to drive,
stumbling down the porch steps to the street.

Not a Word

I don't remember how or where it started
or which of us to blame—I only know it took
a weekend, midsummer, before the silence broke.
We passed each other in the hallways,
our shadows the hue and temper of steel,
and I still feel the jangle of nerves
like a jailor's keys. Had I flirted with—
or even kissed—another woman? Were you
somehow betraying me? You buried yourself
in classics, Eliot and James, while I loitered
on the porch, trying to judge the angles
of rain. I kept waiting for you to launch
some wry remark, about fools who search
for better lives in books they wish they'd written,
about the diaries and albums people box
in attics—explosives ready to trip.
Instead, I cooked, you washed the dishes;
you drove, I pumped the gas.
We sipped each other's cups of trials,
and made them, over time, our own.
We ambled Asia, Europe, shared
many points of concord (though fewer
and fewer, after the first hot years,
of contact). Which is to say, we did our best,
and one damp Saturday and Sunday
refused to speak. Had I made a comment
about the comet of gray streaking your hair?
Or maybe you teased me once too often
about my career as an armchair Marxist
and the image I held sacred of my mother
serving the rich at holiday and wedding fetes—

40

planting hors d'oeuvres with toothpicks
wrapped in colored plastic, *flags*
of the petty bourgeois. I might have frowned
at your morning breath, or coq au vin,
or coldness toward your father's second wife.
Or it could be (and now I am guessing
wildly) I trotted out some dumb pretension
over drinks with guests—concerning, say,
the *fragrantness* of wine—and you,
in that polite little way you had, cleared
your throat and noted: *That's not a word.*

The Village Idiot

The evening your beloved invited you to
vanish, seemingly with no remorse or warning

(how could you sniff at neck and crotch
and fail to catch one whiff of egress?),

and stared with unwarm eyes that hinted,
You perfect dolt, what did you expect?

you wrestled yourself for hours
on the queen-size Perfect Sleeper,

convinced you were the village idiot
of all villages—thatched ones annulled

by fire, or tattooed to a river's arm,
others trembling open legs for thugs.

But then, without warning either, it all
revived: the farmlands of long-forgotten

youth, strung like hammer dulcimers
half in tune, fruit trees skeletal and rheumy

(was it Belarus, eastern France?),
heels of bread you gathered

from the baker's hand and sucked
alone for hours. Trying to rub away

the past, you realized she was right, eerily
precise, again. You saw your father

on a shabby couch, spreading out
his scroll, watermarks at armpits

dark with work, and mother
in a corner of the kitchen, mourning

the knot her womb let slip. With such
a rearing, how could you measure up?

What, indeed, did you expect?
Yet something inside you stirred

at the thought of a sea—there was
a sea!—and woods you stomped in

snow boots, smashing frozen puddles,
courting decades of lousy luck.

You were sick of being poor, sick
for being such, but still held close

the late-March branches, rolling
down their pale green sleeves,

cicadas churning summer down,
haunting bark with crackly ghosts.

And even if you ended up amnesic,
shuffling foreign boulevards

at night, dodging cars and doffing
the dunce caps of streetlamps' cones,

you did find love on one of those
fractured streets. Your dearest lifted

you, cloaked in grime, from the curb,
and offered succor—so, yes, you were

a paramount stooge, but she did take
you up, clearly making her no savant.

III

The Stuff

The night he swerved his roadster down a gully
and phoned me up for help, I drove out ready
to shove him in the mud-slick ditch, spit
in his eye what I knew he knew far better
than any midnight friend—that the stuff
was going to kill him, sooner than later,
maybe someone else, a family perhaps—
but when at last I found him off Highway 5,
chilled and apologetic, under a moth-eaten
blanket of sky, I couldn't bring myself
to scoff or even shake my head,
he seemed so small, far off, as if peered at
through binoculars turned backward.
We stood awhile in silence—he swaying
pinelike, me scanning the pike for cops,
then musing on the muscled vista of black hills.
I could hear the wind leaf nervously
through its books, searching on my behalf
for a timely piece of wisdom that might,
miraculously, cure the man. *I don't know,*
he slurred, *how to thank you,* and I came this
close to snapping *Quit,* but only cracked
a smile—one meant to make me seem too
worldly wise to judge. In fact, I was calling up,
judgmentally, the beer that made him grabby,
wine that stirred up song, the bourbon
with its taste of sun-bleached leather,
tightening the belt. And earlier, I lied.
I rode out planning to bust him once,
sharply in the teeth, to watch blood,
not more regrets, pour from his mouth.

Wasn't that the mouth that told me
I could do anything with my life, anything
on the page? Hadn't he suggested, in writing
of his own, that our spirits are so radiant
they throw shadows of flesh and bone?
Really, he said, *I mean it,* but I could hardly
hear him. Already I was on my back, busy
with chains, hooking them to steel behind
our bumpers, working to pull him free.

Splotches

I sat all morning on the pasture wall
taking the Rorschach tests on flanks
of cows. In one: a team of hikers

at a distance, scaling hills. Another
bore the shadows of shipwreck—
bodies swept to the shore of the visible.

The cows, minding cuds, looked unimpressed.
Same for the flies that nipped at hides.
Then my father reading, not decoding,

the message in the bottle of scotch
flung out by his stranded self.
I caught his drinker's reasoning, circular

as blood. Next came mother's eyes
refusing entry, her dolor rising
like kneaded dough. *What do you*

make of that? I called, but the cows
had slipped away to sip the pond.
Trying to clear my head of those

teasing splotches, I lingered a while
more—then meandered off myself,
humming scraps of half-familiar tunes.

The Lord's Prayer

Understand
how the Lord must feel,
infinite power in each deathless

hand to deal with all
our importunings, pleas for change,
tendered on bended knees.

You too would hesitate
to tamper with creation,
and defer to fate.

Kill off the tyrant—two sprout
from his blood. Dam
with a commandment the raging flood:

soon, the backed-up water
blackens, mosquitoes dip their quills,
publish widespread ills.

To start to edit means never to quit
but to enter the flux
of process, its heave, clever backflips, swirl.

Better to sit and wait—not skim
but neither wrench the text with overreading.
And pray over us like Him.

Instructions for Assembling a Nation

Anything whatsoever may result from anything whatsoever.
—LEV SHESTOV

Bear in mind, shaggy lightning may become a staple food,
or the Shadow Factories drive your GNP—workers
punching in at eight, switching on their toothy machines.

Imagine this patriotic chorus: *A mongrel lifts a leg / pisses on a city wag!*
One necessity, of course, is farming—that and a firm foundation.
Be prepared for *opposniks,* within and without.
Knee-jerks are sure to cry: *Each of us is the other's splint,*
while the self-proclaimed Princes of Stability kick out crutches.

Keep eyes peeled for seditious palindromes—
Pains you cause cause you pains—and all their ilk.

If a man departs his house, barefoot in a yellow robe,
if a dog, tied to a tree, winds itself around and chokes,
draft a constitution. But if the bear-faced architect
buffs a stone, or the small towns of childhood rot;

if someone states, like Laocoön, *A deadly fraud is this,*
and the year becomes a war of spearlike verbs;

if Samuel Beckett drives Andre the Giant to school,
if the self, being all its audiences, packs old wounds in salt;

and the hen turns brown as a barn,
and the sea is a billion windows and a single door,
and that stubby little shit the coccyx demands its rights,

then, and only then, obliterate the bloody thing.

Borges and Himself

In 1946, Juan Perón named Jorge Luis Borges inspector of poultry and rabbits at the Buenos Aires Municipal Market. He refused the post and resigned from government service, condemning the appointment as an unforgivable insult.

I fail to see the libel of surveying beaks and feet,
flattened eyes. Always, Borges: your leathery
ennui (sheath for a polished rage), your pride
that tightens skin until, like a birthday balloon,
it squeaks when rubbed. It might have been a party—
this stint as inspector of meats. Would you, perforce,

have left the arms of jacaranda and rubber trees,
from which the summer shies? Let fade how you
and true love once were each in each, sea and sky?
The carbon dates affirm: that half-life separate
from the gutted, beheaded, and split sums up
your existence. You deserve the wet glove of wind

slapping your cheek. Borges, to purify yourself,
you will need to perform momentous feats of betrayal,
to sneer at avocados, advocates of peace, and start
suspecting cups, rimmed with lipstick in cafés,
of trysts. I doubt you would have lost the libraries,
those oldest, holiest of houses. Or come to forget

that poetry, like poverty, leaves nothing—not necks,
gizzards, or tails—to waste. Surely such a post
would have weighed on you, and yet, like a keystone,
held you firm. I pity you more than beasts who poke
and squirm. Borges, you and I never touched,
but floated through like twins in vitro—time

and the scrim of selfhood between. Unlike you,
arriving from work, I peel off the placenta of clothes.
The sweat stains conjure blood, surrendered in
provision's name. I seek to distill myself almost
to nil, so in the end, my absence will scarcely fill
an absinthe glass—a cinch for loved ones to drain.

Menelaus

was the kind of guy who could eat
with gusto
and never grow fat.

Like the past.

Wiry.

Like dreams of the piano tuner's wife.

Able to hoist, antlike,
many times
his mass.

I fell
for his wife, not hard enough to break a rib,
but still.

At parties, she would perch on the edge of a couch, sip
sloe gin fizzes, carefully slice
open a feeling, and read it out loud—
her voice like dusk
rising to claim a field

of troops.

Prodigal Son

Father the pepper, mother the grinder.
Mother the salt, father the egg.
Winds shredding bolt after bolt of cloud.

Brother the mole, plowing below the plow.
Sister reading but disavowing Stein.
There's no here here, she intones, mimicking the mystics.

I'm not about to curl, grow crooked with aestivation.
The bone cries white, cries stone; the deep pulse taps.
Forget the cistern water, bird-milk cakes.

Soothsayers promise a long run
in which we'll be better off. But the wrong boy stole
my sister's hand, and she waved it leaving town.

Envy stabs me now, and whose face doesn't hang
on hinges, isn't many half-closed doors?
The brook keeps on explaining: *To be is to be disappointed*

and to disappoint. Yet I have nothing to fear or lose.
Streets lead only to other streets, and just this morning I discovered
a wrinkled twenty in a pair of jeans just washed.

To a Fool

Because you reproached a younger man
for being foolish, not respecting foolishness
as the sacred province of younger men,
and because this insult turned you into,
once again, one of those naïve clowns,
I have come to recommend the thicket
of stars and fox-eyed planets glaring
down; because you chewed and swallowed,
spoke out of turn, instead of savoring
on your tongue the wafer of hesitation,
I have traveled streets full of cavities
and loose fillings to reveal the hickories
that open shutters, hurl stones at passersby.
The cosmos has quit shooting for the day
its documentary *Blue Circus.* The spider
ceases plucking its carnivorous harp.
But because you shamed a younger man
last night, in front of his new wife,
because you moved his face to a place
of disgrace, I have left the stunned
palm in the corner of my office,
with its dark green shock of hair,
to summon continental shelves
grinding teeth in ocean depths,
and the shoebox full of shadows
you found one spring in attic dust.
Among the shuffle came not
the sun-haired girl of your dreams
who never balked, but the bloated

one of nightmare, rising from silt
with open arms to draw you close.
You, a much younger man
at the time, and a patent fool.

I Should Be Livid

With water in my lungs I come, with two ring fingers
and kneecaps shaved by grit,

I come with special knowledge:
the heart has no fields
but it does
no medicinal herbs or poppies bloom there
but they do.

I should be livid

for you wedged yourself between me
and the mausoleums of beehives
and the sheet music on the flanks of trout
you brushed aside the lizard
prizing open dawn.

I am certain you made a clod of me
letting the woos go on
after the blood had cooled—damn I see now
we were tourists of affection, never true inhabitants of that storied realm,
never citizens in the . . . wait, life's too short for prose.

I still miss your jutting second toes.
Like oceans though
we must make visible only
a fraction of our losses, grind them into sandy coasts.

I should be livid yet

after parting I did not feel

like a current inside
large water, alive but bound on every side, or used by you,

who surely rode me in leisure for a time
before tying to a sturdy dock.

Bread

When you bake an excellent bread
and the crust comes hard—dark brown
and flaky, the sesame seeds dark brown—
that is a good day. I say it again.
The morning you bake a superior bread
and the smell wafts through the house,
inhabiting rooms like Victoria's God,
that is the start of a very good day.

But when the dough collapses, dryly
breaks apart, when salt or yeast controls,
then we live where only jagged coastlines
record the rhythms of the ocean's heart.
Lunches become a wheat field, mustard field,
and pig farm slammed together.

There is one constant: everything and nothing changes
all at once all the time. When baking falters,
passion turns to service, and you dispense
with hygiene, wear instead
a shadow face. You amputate
the bread in slices, and hill men trudge
their musty paths through daughters.
Lives explode into coin.

On days when bread comes perfect though,
Good morning, you say, *beautiful heavy anything.*
And before you know it, someone's ear receives
a life story from your mouth—the very mouth
you feed good bread, piping hot.

Correspondent

They demanded lacerations, the snapping of spines
     like whips. You gave connotations—yellow and below
          the surface, mild bruises. They called for welts,

pillows in which pain conceals its face, for faces
     with the paleness of fired dung. You dug instead
          for the real war news, eternally unpublished,

about hope attacking the poor, in tireless campaigns,
     dropping shells from pulpits, platforms festooned
          with visages and flags. What bunk about the Old Life,

they complained, mocking recollection as a trick
     of rapid-eye sleep. They wanted ledes on bandits,
          opening the night with pry bars, on bitterness infusing

the polis—an iodine drip. But you took flight to report
     on quiet, scrabble-familiar folks, ready to die for Mother
          Russia, birdless Guam. You chose to cover stop signs

on perpetual strike, marching in place, placards raised.
     Give us pouches of sleeplessness, they croaked,
          beneath a youthful widow's eyes. Where are the child

soldiers, sheltered under salutes? Hegel, they insisted,
     called history monochromatic, splashed in red.
          Enough of subtle shades. Yet what about the immigrant

heart, you wondered, ready to reshape the world?
     Where is it written that the innocent must live off
          miracles and rice? Then again, where is it not?

They commissioned profiles: kids of the wildly rich,
        in stupors of proper comportment; you scribbled
                notes on guests adopting poses, doodled portraits

of the duchess of ruin, who tithed too much.
        Settling a half mile inland, where all the seawords end,
            you wrote, read, watched inspired films.

Is anybody home, anyone living? They stipulated
        headlines unambiguously bold, scratched
            your sidebars on the adequate amounts of time

to ponder the time remaining. Of course, in the end,
        they broke you. One summer in the field, you dreamt
            of making love to death, its lips touched lightly to yours.

Why can't you see the adverb, they barked,
        for the cheap prosthesis it is? What's this business
            in paragraph three: *my figurine, fig, my sunken pumpkin?*

How would it be if the ages could open and close,
        not like iron gates but gills of fish? What if cloud banks
            didn't hover like souls of dying continents?

They wanted lungs of army tents collapsing,
        posh golf fairways hacked from their Platonic forms.
            And now you are drifting off, leaving us to long

for the perfect memories of snapshots, so we might tear
        the past to pieces, feed it to the wind. Far off, a car
            burns rubber. Its skid marks must resemble smeared

mascara of a mother's eyes. There were wooden
        crates with wares, water gray as lead. Long arms tensed
            their cordage. They commanded that you show them

towns, ripening then rotting on a river's branch,
  doctors inured to anguish, anesthetized by school.
    These are the stories we are born and banished into,

they explained, the ones with contusion stains
  of berries on the palm. But all those palms,
    you countered, are mapped with dead-end roads.

You recorded the dove's apologia,
  admired the willow's floor-length skirts.
    In our winter bones we understood. They wanted

lash marks of arid creeks, minds like scattered
  leaves. This flash of afternoon, that sunrise a shock.
    Front lawns blue and barely breathing. The grass,

it looked afraid. We must be grass in part.
  Your hours, as we supposed, were awful,
    paychecks worse. First frost, they cut you loose.

IV

Man of Feeling

This morning my heart goes out to pines
punctured and slung with hammocks
in leisure's name, to the redbird
with its bandit mask, accused of every crime.
I feel bonded all at once to dogs
on chains, reciting prison
diaries as I pass; suddenly I open
to the possum, ugly as the trash it picks.
Soon I will return to selfish queries:
What trophies have I stowed in cabinets?
How many rivers forked at my birth?
But today I want to harry vapid
questions—as smaller, quicker birds
do hawks and crows—want to be overcome
by clotheslines pinned with cast-off
selves, my mouth blowing ovals of awe.
For years I could not care less
that the turtle and armadillo carry
caskets on their backs the span
of their lives, that the spider quilts
in a solitude so consuming it devours
what guests drop by. Yet warmth has found
an entrance, or picked some shackle inside,
and I even feel for kudzu, choking all.
Earlier this summer, without a qualm,
I bagged and dragged to the curb
a goose found floating in the boat slip,
made crude by some Evinrude or Merc.
But now as the sun bobs up, I might be
an earl in the Age of Reason, so completely
have I fallen under sympathy's sway.

I hum in chorus with the mournful woodwinds
of rotted elms. And face with desperate
affection the stucco homes—guarded,
blank—like the man I was just yesterday,
who welcomes, least of any, my embrace.

Interlude

I let myself grow bottom heavy, like a cello,
and droned low noise. My nerves had given me,
to use your phrase, *the anus of an apple,*

and a face lit only in parts—like an office high-rise
or hospital at night. But you insisted I am just
as deathless as any rock or shell, and warned me

to doubt the clocks for keeping time an exhibition
behind glass. The past and future, you said,
are always equidistant, proving we cycle through,

not streak. All the same, I peered down rails for pain,
as for a scheduled train, and scratched reviews
of books *overlong but touched, like gladiolas,*

with lavish buds. Had you never clutched me
on that street in Brighton Beach, or stated flatly,
narrow-eyed, that men who run in circles surge

into tornadoes, I would still be lauding the suicidal—
gaunt ones wrung by love, gulping the berries of pills;
those who wince on a razor's ledge, then plunge.

Ever since, each puddle seems a novice ocean,
no longer a shallow grave of storm, and I covet less
the grace of the martins' predation, the dandelion

midsummer—its head in the cloud of its head.
I'll always favor suites of darker tone, but lately
I can grin when you insist we drive, unreasonably

out of our way, to purchase gas at a truck stop by
the name of Love's. And eagerly, I hear crickets reach
crescendo, love, before stowing their violas in the grass.

Mine

Praise to the drowsy houseflies of September,
to smokestacks belching wealth, janitors
who broom errata into mounds. Honor broken
wall clocks in their comas, potted plants
of the elderly and ill, untended but content
in bathrobes of dust. I have learned
from deciduous trees, stacking pyres
to summer's demise, have studied
my Italian nana at her altar—two blue
halos lit, frying peppers and onions,
stirring sauce. For months I roamed
the maze of an absent lover's thumbprint.
Weeks flaked off the calendar, whitewash
from a weathered fence, and every night
in sleep, I kissed her lips' wrinkle
of doubt. I was torpid, folded inward.
Yet you hammered planks across the trunks
of trees, somehow coaxed me to climb.
So now I salute the prairies humming
with wind, the deceitful ecosystem
in my boyhood box of tackle,
on which I might have blamed so much.
I celebrate discordant birds, nasty music
strung on power lines, even forgive the cop
who bruised my brother with a nightstick,
simply for playing Feste in the street.
But most of all I praise the city, our city,
from a favorite lookout, spread before us
like a sidewalk vendor's sprawl of gewgaws—
or mine, dear, of precious stones.

Love to Death

They will say you go together
like a lid and canning jar,
chopsticks, or a lock and key.
They'll speak of the groom
as a decent chap, come at last
to his senses, and compliment
the bride—her hips recalling
an oil lamp, slender shoulders
those of the violin.

Because I cannot make it
(forgive me for living
an eighth of the world away),
no one there will mention
gray hills crouched in rain, delta
basins clogged with sloughed-off
skins of rivers, or talk of night
in its threadbare jacket,
the half-devoured biscuit of the moon.

As soon as cocktails commence,
couples will let their eyes swim
back to the Summer of Love, trill
a few bars of Dylan, then call to mind
park benches, trunks of trees,
where their initials heal to this day.
Not one will recollect the anomie,
passed around like weed, or grease
making string of their hair, none

will state that newlyweds are dice,
tossed into love and tumbling
all the way, with any luck, to death.
One time, at a large reception,
a father giving his daughter away
announced that he loved her
to death. My wife, the Russian,
turned to me with a face
that asked, *to death?*

Later, when the music and dancing
die, aunts and uncles, siblings
and old friends, will cluster
at the end of the bar to sing
your most laughable gaffes:
how one of you blanched a spot
on the lawn, splashing gasoline,
how the other (tipsy) tried to guess
what morning glories issue

from their horns. And then,
if their love is true, these guests
will chime your consolations:
that the light of long-dead stars
still reaches us, if God's cannot,
that each day closes from the top,
like a window shade, lending us
the privacy to strip and take the oaths
that emblazon and raze our lives.

Don't you say in English: shoot
to death? strangle to death?
beat? bore? So wondered
in a whisper my pepper
speck, poppy seed, period
at the close of single life.

What will I ever do with her,
who sprinkles salt on slugs
that gnaw her pansies, who *seasons*

them to death—almost giddy
as they writhe? I liked it better
when she murdered by night
with tins of beer they can't deny—
Miller High Life, Milwaukee's Best—
slugging swill the whole way down.
But times like this demand champagne.
Let's raise our glasses then, miles
apart, and strip from our minds

the little frights—sunrise a blunt
head trauma gauzed in fog; ruined
birds at a picture window's feet.
(Maybe that's the way to gloss
our *love to death:* adoration
that flies full speed, unaware
and unafraid of what's ahead.)
It's late, and I am sleepy.
The goldfish across the room

ogles me, repeating a phrase
I can't make out, though it looks
like the drawn, imploring *Let's GO*
my wife will mouth from across
the room, halfway through a boring
party. Let's toast the demise
of boring parties, birth of a lively
marriage. I wish I could be
in attendance. Truly, I do.

If Only

If only you had won
that contest of jabs, that game
of blackjack, that job.
If only stars looked more
like words than punctuation,
and night less
like a battered shield.

Maybe then you could relax
in recollection, if only you hadn't missed
that train, that missive
and miraculous chance. One day,
rinsed in sun, you stroll
a market palming melons, nosing
where umbilicals snapped,

the next, you browse memorial
parks, shopping for the crown
of your demise. Like the Buddhist,
all you wanted was to want
nothing, and like the starlet
to be wanted, and like the addict
to say, for once, *I won't.*

If only you could join the moths,
disciples of flame, and think of pupils
as eclipses, blotting inner light.
Why continue to mutter through
the weighty grays of rain? Why search
for truths in neighbors' windows,
when every answer is a silhouette?

Each night, you sleep beside me—
my smarter, better-looking
double—and dream of children
we'll either have or have to
become. It needn't be that way.
If only the backs of arches didn't ache
from monuments and bridges,

if only we could all shake hands
with gusto, but keep our treaties unsigned.
Perhaps we wouldn't flinch at lightning,
even the charges trapped in sixty-watt bulbs.
If only the heart were not a hive
of angry tenants, and birthmarks
what remain of former lives: the scars.

Marriage

If you'll please jab with a stick
and garden-hose clean
the dog do on my sneaker,
then I will gladly answer

queries about the cotton
farms I worked as a girl
in the Soviet south. I know
Americans see history

as cinematic—technicolored,
with boomy surround sound—
look how they plop in front
of enormous screens, munch

on simulations of life.
Soviet, as you know, means
wise counsel, but I prefer
to keep our arrangement

quid pro quo (a fancy name
for sex). If you'll steer me
from men made out of noise
and sport, and acknowledge

that a sheer rain peers
at me now, a rain of infinite
glances, then I promise not
to balk when you speak of Vulcan,

mallets in your neck and wrists,
I swear to switch the topic
when a slip of tongue reveals
your memory still a sponge,

heavy with your first wife's name.
I can honor any good man's
madness, but it means you must
refrain from thinking of the dead

as sunken treasure, and snuff
your fatherly guides (cinder heads,
you've said yourself). Do this,
and I will never stagger toward you,

brandishing a broken oath,
gripped like a busted bottle
in a Hollywood brawl, slash
the air near your face.

You claim poetry peculiar,
having to be half asleep to do
the job. But the same goes
for the hospital floors—all

those aches and worries,
recollections: cabins steeped
in fog, kites and planets
snagging trees a life ago.

Here is the body of lead,
the patients point, here
of burns, there the one
once tossed with glee in a stream.

If you will save me from
these wrecks when I come
home, and go on
chanting the living things

(hermit crab the scrivener,
the great society of grass),
then I will stretch out
bones and thump a beat.

I am sorry, dear, to refuse
to smoke your "grass,"
but this is marriage, and I am
used to choosing different

forms of numbness. For us,
it was vodka, vodka. Still,
I adore the sound and shape
of grass, and would love to learn

how it remembers: yielding
to the other's weight and holding
the impression. If you will let me
count the sorrows in the lawn

after you mow, if you'll drive us
to the scalloped sea, so we can
watch the sun blot out the coast,
then I will excuse the strange

calamity in the row house
of your youth, and drop
the bag-lady chuckle
when you botch my tongue.

Have I mentioned my linguist friend
from Samarkand? In school,
she spread on the couch, late at night,
listing not the parts of speech,

but the segments of a wished-for
speaker—a loquacious, athletic lover,
sauntering the Silk Road.
I loved the way she dreamed,

with perfect candor, grammar.
Arm in arm along that route,
we wondered which came first,
oligarch or goony mob,

suspecting they were thrown,
both at once, like dice.
Their snake eyes glare without
a mote of grace. I miss Tatyana

every day, yet I was in a rush
to show my parents what
I could do: more than grow
hair long for sale to weavers.

I have turned, you know, a corner
or two, discovered other
hard right angles. Maybe
once a life, twice perhaps,

you're real. Let's purchase,
then, a plot in an unmarked field
and have our bodies buried
without coffins. I am ready

to wait eternity for dogs
to mingle our bones in play.
One night, we were going down
again, in a flood of fire,

First Husband and I, First Cause.
And by the speckled quail
of the dusk you love, I swear
I wanted never to return.

I could not recognize my life
as a self-inflicted, comic gaffe—
like swinging at a gnat and smacking
your own face instead. I was slapstick

roundabout carousel ruin.
But you stirred out of nowhere,
like branches making visible
the wind, and I could tell the things

you didn't hold inside your head—
the slow erasure of the female,
the power, ardor of it.
I would shudder if I caught myself

wishing for some softness under
gray-walled skies, but you urged
me to bite the plum, and made me
(it's just this simple) laugh.

I smelled books on you,
and the scent recalled my first
slovar. I took you, like it, to bed,
opened your covers in lamplight.

It was a gorgeous night outside,
outside apprehension, and you
showed no dark intent.
If you can do just that, the rest

of our time, then I will do my best
to veer from droppings of mutts
on my morning strolls,
and choose when I shop for you

shirts of only high-grade cotton.
I will be *more than happy,*
as you Americans say, to shuffle
in a line outside the movies,

late November, and name the shapes
that leak from our mouths.
More than happy—as if joy
alone were not enough.

White Night on the Neva

To the one in steel-gray trousers,
tambourine deaf, you refused to wave
a surrendering skin. Awestruck
as a sunflower, you slipped off

far from him. A poplar cast
the lightning of its shadow
on crabgrass patched with snow,
and your face diverged at mine.

I have yet to learn the Russian names
for weather, though we have swayed
beyond the forecasts. First a stroll
beside the river tugging itself to sea,

all streetlamps moot. Then, at midnight,
we watched tomorrow stop
to preen in the wrinkled mirror,
before leaping into yesterday.

Even though the skies blacken sooner
these miles and years from then, today
we trace another water's edge. Today,
which I have come to call *sevodyna*.

After the Miscarriage

It faded bit by bit in a garden pail
my wife prepared with towels.

She cleansed the wound, daubed
head and beak, she coaxed.

Hours later the bird still jerked,
its life an inch too wide to fit its fate.

Then, as dusk came on, it quit.
I lack a soul, it seems. My thought

from the start: take the spade,
lift the chick from its mantle

of ants, gently feed a hole out back.
I spoke about a misery—timeless,

abstract—out of which we should
put the thing. Slack-winged,

vaguely blue, it must have been
pecked just short of death

by a parent long on mouths to fill.
Or gouged by some mortal foe.

Yet wouldn't hawk or owl
have hauled it off?

First Night Alone with Twins

We laughed,
we wept, saw
visions. Regained
our faith in God,
renounced His salves
again. More visions.

The night was Dickensian—
sweeping and full
of social import—then
Dickinsonian, sweaty,
cramped, riddled
with doubt.

If only we had one.

If only a third arrived.

A silent toast to the pomegranate,
belly aching with seed.
Mute cheers for the woman
on my block growing up
who bore eleven kids—
two slid back out of time.

A cooling mist of giggles.
Torrential ululations and skirls.
Scenes by Hieronymus Bosch.

We beamed the broad
dumb smiles of picket

fences, stared ahead
with hollow eyes
like Victorian foreclosures.

A longing to escape
forever, deep wish
never to move.

Rockwell
oiled out by Pollock.

And dawn brought
revelation: two
of them were clearly
too much to hold.

We didn't let go.

The End

In the end it would all work out,
all work out in the end. Zebras,
blameless from the egg, would strip

away their inmate clothes,
and the boy next door stop pelting
ducks with stones. It would be fruitful

in the end, the horizon roused
from trance, the poet's spouse
steering a yacht after all that gloom.

In the end we would rear up
like goats on spindles, and launch
parades, our pasts no longer

rooms of echoes circling our names.
We would lower into salted baths,
as the old intelligence of silence

reigned supreme. If only the end
had not been born with the beginning,
its fraternal twin. We could conjure

infancy with ease, days of supping
on our mothers, keep secrets out
of sight, packed up high in elms.

Once we walked the Neva, you and I,
then spun and spun in labyrinthine
Venice. Now we cling but can't stop

falling into what we were. You fix
your hair in the bathroom, I sit
at my desk and type. I lie. I always

lie and only sometimes type.
What a helpless lot we are, simple
and lazy, even if we mastered flight.

Leaning wheat and soiled kerchief,
slumped shoulders of distant hills:
nothing would be dismissed in the end,

not one thing cast away. Trees
astir with contemplation, terns
that loot. In the end it would all

work out, all abide. Rivers
would press their mouths to seas
and go on nursing, if the end

were more than myth, or less.
You would hold a crocus to one ear,
and listen beyond the fractious

to a chorus bent on cure.
I would stand chest deep in traffic,
ignoring the profanities and horns.